PIANO/VOCAL

Selections for

"damn yankees"

ISBN 978-1-4950-9366-1

HAL•LEONARD®
7777 W. Bluemound Rd. P.O. Box 13819 Milwaukee, WI 53213

In Australia Contact:
Hal Leonard Australia Pty. Ltd.
4 Lentara Court
Cheltenham, Victoria, 3192 Australia
Email: ausadmin@halleonard.com.au

Visit Hal Leonard Online at
www.halleonard.com

3   **The Game**

16   **Goodbye, Old Girl**

20   **Heart**

24   **A Little Brains, A Little Talent**

33   **Near to You**

38   **Shoeless Joe from Hannibal, Mo.**

42   **Six Months Out of the Year**

56   **Those Were the Good Old Days!**

60   **Two Lost Souls**

64   **Whatever Lola Wants (Lola Gets)**

67   **Who's Got the Pain?**

THE GAME

Words and Music by RICHARD ADLER
and JERRY ROSS

8

GOODBYE, OLD GIRL

Words and Music by RICHARD ADLER
and JERRY ROSS

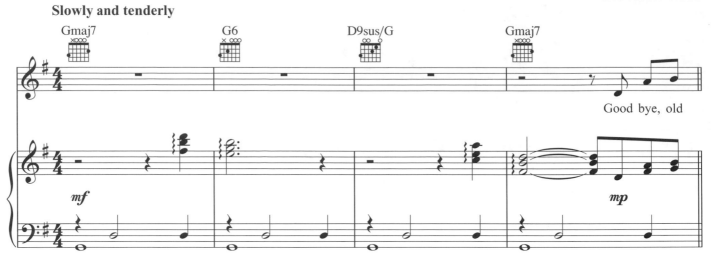

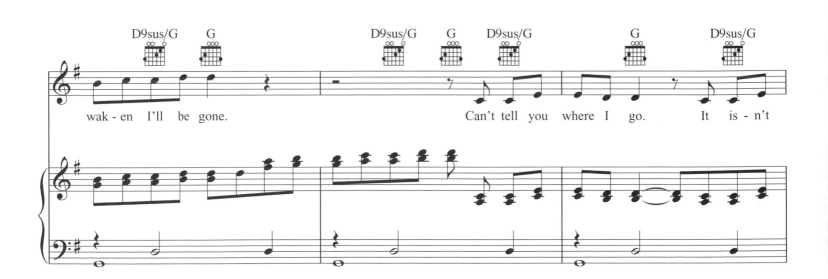

HEART

Words and Music by RICHARD ADLER
and JERRY ROSS

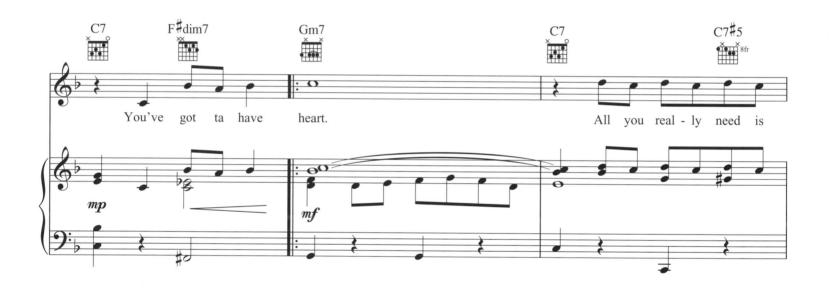

You've got ta have heart. All you real-ly need is

heart. When the odds are say-in' you'll nev-er win, __

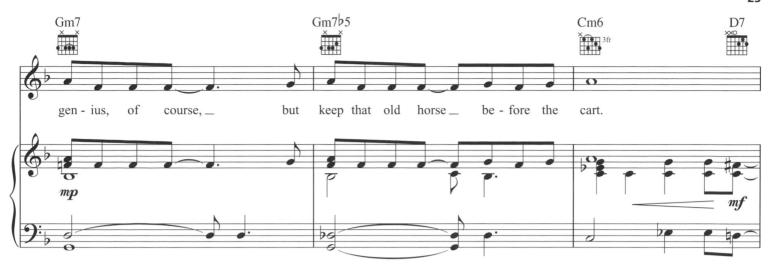

gen - ius, of course, ___ but keep that old horse ___ be - fore the cart.

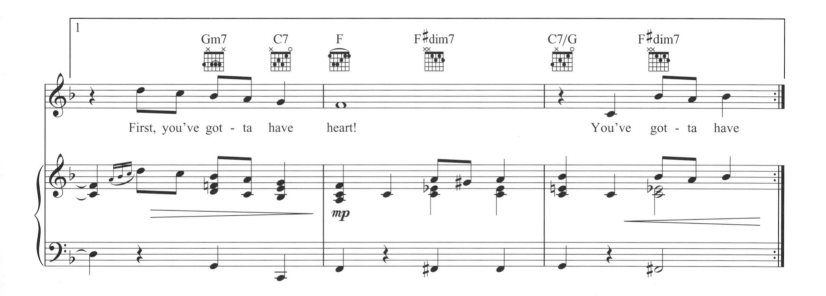

First, you've got - ta have heart! You've got - ta have

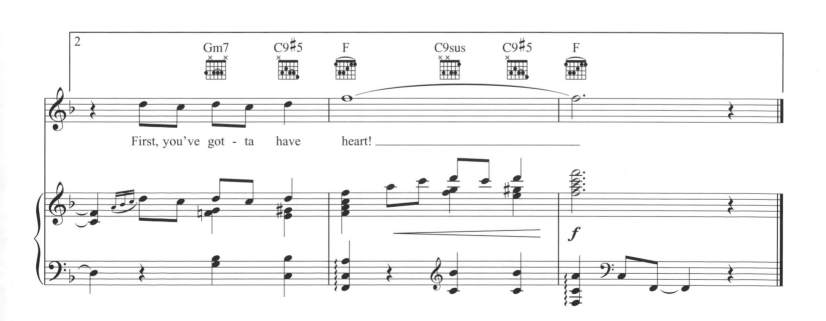

First, you've got - ta have heart! _____

A LITTLE BRAINS, A LITTLE TALENT

Words and Music by RICHARD ADLER
and JERRY ROSS

25

NEAR TO YOU

Words and Music by RICHARD ADLER
and JERRY ROSS

34

SHOELESS JOE
FROM HANNIBAL, MO.

Words and Music by RICHARD ADLER
and JERRY ROSS

SIX MONTHS OUT OF THE YEAR

Words and Music by RICHARD ADLER
and JERRY ROSS

46

THOSE WERE THE GOOD OLD DAYS!

Words and Music by RICHARD ADLER
and JERRY ROSS

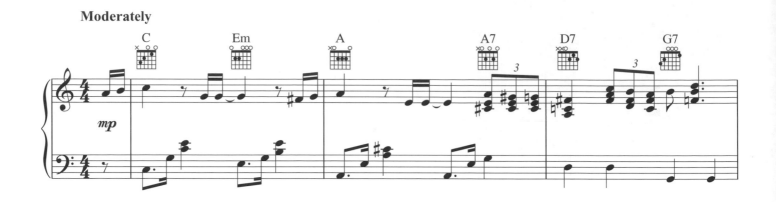

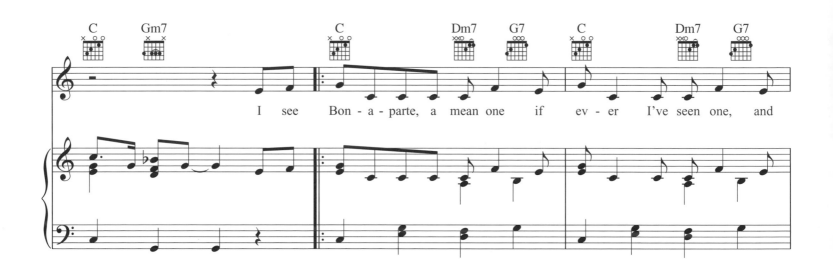

I see Bon - a - parte, a mean one if ev - er I've seen one, and

Ne - ro fid - dlin' through that love - ly blaze. An - toi - nette, dain - ty queen, with her

57

TWO LOST SOULS

Words and Music by RICHARD ADLER
and JERRY ROSS

WHATEVER LOLA WANTS
(Lola Gets)

Words and Music by RICHARD ADLER
and JERRY ROSS

Whatever Lola wants _____ Lola gets, _____

_____ and, little man, little Lola wants you.

Make up your mind to have _____ no regrets. _____

WHO'S GOT THE PAIN?

Words and Music by RICHARD ADLER
and JERRY ROSS